DEDICATION

To the members of my first critique group,
"The Butt in Chair Group,"
who taught me most of what I
know about critique groups:

Cathleen Armstrong, Laurie Kehler, Kathi
Lipp, Barbara Milligan, Judy Squier, Debbie
Turnrose, Katie Vorieter, Kathie Williams

To the members of my present critique group,

"Warrior Women Writers,"
who continue to teach me:

Gabriela Banks, Laurie Kehler, Christi Naler,
Stephanie Shoquist

and to Elizabeth Thompson
who co-taught this material with
me for so many years.

CRITIQUE GROUPS THAT WORK

A HANDBOOK FOR STARTING, LEADING, & PARTICIPATING IN A CHRISTIAN WRITERS CRITIQUE GROUP

PAT J. SIKORA

MIGHTY OAK
MINISTRIES

Redwood City, CA

Pat J. Sikora—Mighty Oak Ministries

For more resources and free downloads to help your writing career, go to:

Website: mightyoakministries.com
Email: pats@mightyoakministries.com
Facebook: facebook.com/mightyoakministries

CRITIQUE GROUPS THAT WORK!
A Handbook for Starting,
Leading, & Participating in a Christian Writers Critique Group

Copyright © 2006, 2018 by Pat J. Sikora

ISBN-13 978-1-947877-00-9 paperback
ISBN-13: 978-1-947877-01-6 e-book

Library of Congress Control Number: 2017918379

Mighty Oak Ministries, Redwood City, CA

Cover and Interior Design: Jose Pepito Jr.

Printed in the United States of America

All Scripture quotations unless otherwise indicated, are taken from *Holy Bible, New International Version®, NIV®* Copyright ©1973, 1978, 1984, 2011 by Biblica, Inc.® Used by permission. All rights reserved worldwide.

For citations on additional Scripture translations, see the Bibliography.

All Internet addresses (websites, etc.) in this book are offered as a resource. They are not intended in any way to be or imply an endorsement by the author or Mighty Oak Ministries, nor does Mighty Oak Ministries vouch for the content of these sites for the life of this book.

CONTENTS

INTRODUCTION

Is It Time for A Critique Group?

The muse hits and you pound the computer well into the night. Or while the kids are napping. Or on your lunch hour.

You know you're a writer because you can't *not* write. You've had stories in your soul from childhood. And now, finally, you're birthing them.

But are they any good? Do they speak to anyone other than you and your cat?

There you sit, alone with your computer. Typing. Deleting. Typing again. Shaping words into sentences, sentences into paragraphs, paragraphs into chapters. And then it's done. Now what?

Some writers are content to simply put the words on the page. A cathartic process that brings solace to the soul, healing to the spirit, clarity to the confusion.

But others want to share their writing with the world. They want to publish. And when writing turns from hobby to profession, even a tentative profession, it may be time to bring others into the process. It may be time to join or start a critique group.

A critique group can help you get started, stay engaged, and finish well. A critique group can help you polish your work and find a publisher. A critique group can help you determine what type of writing you're best at.

And perhaps most important, a critique group can support you, encourage you, and pray with you. Your critique group will rejoice with you when you make a sale or nail a rewrite. They'll cry with you when you receive those inevitable rejections, and they'll be the ones to pick you up, brush you off, and get you writing again. If you're a writer, you know about the solitary life. Now it's time to learn about the shared life.

This book is aimed at Christian writers, and suggests that you will benefit from a Christian group. However, we will also discuss other options. Only you know what will be best for you and your style of writing.

So let's look at what you can gain from a critique group and how to get started.

We are coworkers belonging to God…
(1 Corinthians 3:9)

SOME PRELIMINARIES

What is a Critique Group?

C ritique groups can take a variety of forms, many of which we'll discuss in this book. The form you select will depend on what is available near you, your personality, and the time you have available.

Simply stated, *a critique group is a place to share your writing with the specific purpose of honing your skills and making your manuscript publication-ready.* As a bonus, a critique group will provide you with support and encouragement in a lonely profession.

Let's face it. We all think our writing is perfect. Or we think it's terrible. The reality is probably somewhere in between, but we'll never know that unless we share our writing with others.

John McPhee, writer for *The New Yorker* and author of 38 books, says, "If you lack confidence in setting one word after another and sense that you are stuck in a place from which you will never be set free, if you feel sure that you will never make it and were not cut out to do this, if your prose seems stillborn and you completely lack confidence, you must be a writer."[1] And I would add, you need a critique group to spur you on.

A critique group is a safer place to debut your work than sending it directly to a publisher. And the end-product after several people have had eyes on your piece will almost always be better than what you can produce alone.

I differentiate between a writers' group and a critique group, although the difference is slight. Typically, writers' groups are aimed at improving writing skills, and networking, but not necessarily critiquing your work. They are wonderful for hobbyists or for professionals wanting to meet other writers.

A critique group, on the other hand, is usually aimed at making your writing publication-ready. You will want to decide on your purpose before beginning since it can be frustrating to have some members

---

[1]   John McPhee, *Draft. No. 4 : On the Writing Process*, First edition. ed. (New York: Farrar, Straus and Giroux, 2017), 158.

treating their writing as a hobby and others treating it as a profession. This distinction will be important in both the skills and support functions of the group.

This book will focus on critique groups for writers seeking publication.

I had been writing professionally for more than twenty years before I was invited to join my first critique group. We met regularly for about ten years. Some members came and went, but the core members were active for the whole time. When we started, I was the only published author. Over the years, almost every person who invested a few years in the group either had their work traditionally published or self-published. There have been at least 27 books from the six most active members, with publications continuing long after the group dissolved. Recently I started a new group comprised of five women who met at a writers' conference. We used this book to structure and form our group.

In addition to my firsthand knowledge, I've gleaned information and insights from several other groups and have taught this material as a workshop at various writers' conferences for many years, either alone or with Elizabeth Thompson (ElizabethMThompson. com) who founded Inspire Christian Writers (inspirewriters.com) in northern California. In the process, I gained insights from her and from workshop attendees who do their groups differently than we managed ours.

Rejoice with those who rejoice; mourn with those who mourn.
(Romans 12:15)

Benefits of a Critique Group

There are many benefits of participating in a critique group. Let's look at some of them.

- ➢ **To gain the collective wisdom and perspective of others regarding your writing.**

  - A good critique group can help you accentuate your positives and correct your negatives.

  - A good critique group can help you understand how various readers will interpret what you thought was utterly clear.

  - A good critique group can help you improve your writing and marketing skills.

  - A good critique group can help you learn to "write tight," which is what every editor is looking for.

- ➢ **To develop a network of people who speak your language and understand your**

heartbeat, perhaps even more than your family can.

- A good critique group will rejoice with your successes and weep with your rejections.

- A good critique group understands the fear of putting your heart on paper, only to be rejected, and they understand the joy of publication.

- A good critique group offers fellowship, support, and prayer with like-minded people.

➢ **To help novice writers develop their craft.**

- A good critique group of experienced writers may want to include beginners as a ministry.

- A good critique group of beginning writers can grow and develop their skills together as they become excellent. Our first group consisted primarily of beginners when we started.

➢ **To help authors build their platform and help with marketing, both of which are critical in today's market.**

- A good critique group can review your blog posts, website content, and marketing materials.

- A good critique group can brainstorm suggestions for marketing your books and can share resources for marketing.

- A good critique group can cooperate in cross-promoting members and their work on blogs, podcasts, and social media.

---

*We...pray that our God will make you fit
for what he's called you to be,
pray that he'll fill your good ideas and acts of faith
with his own energy
so that it all amounts to something.*
(2 Thessalonians 1:11 MSG)

Types of Critique Groups

ritique groups come in all shapes and sizes, but can generally be classified as "in-person" or "on-line." These groups will share many features, but each will also have a unique character.

IN-PERSON GROUPS

As the name suggests, these groups meet in person in a pre-defined location and at a pre-defined time. They are a meeting you need to attend. You have to show up.

This is my preference, despite the disadvantages. Most of this book focuses on this type of group. In-person groups can be further segmented into those that read in the group meeting and those that read in advance, bringing critiques to the meeting for discussion. These differences will be discussed in the section "Decide How You Will Present Material, p. 49."

Let's look at the advantages and disadvantages of in-person vs. online groups.

TABLE 1: ADVANTAGES AND DISADVANTAGES
OF IN-PERSON GROUPS

ADVANTAGES	DISADVANTAGES
Meet local writers. Writing is a lonely profession. While it's important to keep your "butt in chair" and write, sometimes it's good to get out and talk with other human beings.	**Sometimes it's difficult to find enough local writers to form an effective group.** In many geographic areas, there simply aren't enough writers, especially Christian writers, to form a group. You may be further limited by the caliber of writers in the area or what type of group is available. **Lack of specialization** can be a problem if you write a genre that has unique needs.
Critiques are generally kinder, more gracious, when done in person. Sometimes, especially today, it's just too easy to be unkind when responding online.	**Criticism can be harder to take face-to-face.** It's difficult to hear criticism of your work and it's hard to fight the urge to argue. (But it's a skill you need to develop.)

ADVANTAGES	DISADVANTAGES
You will develop new and often lifelong relationships. Many of the members of your group will become close friends.	**Personality conflicts** are harder to deal with in person. Comments can seem personal. But again, this is a professional skill to develop.
Get fresh reactions and feedback. Especially where you read your manuscript in the group, you can watch and listen for the reactions of your fellow writers. Do they fidget? Laugh? Gasp? Fall asleep? You can only get such insights from reading to a group.	**Meetings are scheduled events** and you are expected to adjust your schedule to accommodate them.
You can discuss problems you are having with your manuscript. Sometimes you just need to brainstorm with someone who understands writing or can bring a different perspective.	**Sometimes it's easy to talk and talk rather than write and write.** While brainstorming can be useful, don't let it take the place of writing.

ADVANTAGES	DISADVANTAGES
You develop a thicker professional skin. Writers are often sensitive folks. We don't want anyone calling our baby ugly. But if we want to develop as professionals, sometimes we need to hear the truth and learn how to receive critique professionally. It isn't easy, but better to hear it from friends than in a rejection letter.	**It's easy to negatively compare our skills with those of others.** That's human nature, and it can either lead to our growth or our negative self-esteem.

ONLINE GROUPS

Online groups are becoming more popular with easily available Internet. These groups usually form around a central person or website. A variation on these include Facebook closed groups. Members submit their writing for critique on their time schedule and get critiques at the convenience of the members. Each group may determine their own rules.

TABLE 2: ADVANTAGES AND DISADVANTAGES OF ONLINE GROUPS

ADVANTAGES	DISADVANTAGES
You may interact with writers from around the world. Since you aren't limited by geography or time zone, you can meet and develop friendships with writers anyplace.	**You don't really get to know the people in your group.** They are usually just a name and a manuscript unless someone reaches out for in-real-life contact.
On-line groups can be more specialized, focusing on a specific genre or target audience.	**There is more fear of others stealing your work.** This is often a concern of beginning writers, but it is more of a possibility when there is no face to face contact or even a way of contacting a person who goes dark.

ADVANTAGES	DISADVANTAGES
You may get more honest feedback since the relationship is more distant. Your critique partner is reacting only to your writing, not your looks, your personality, or your friendship. This is generally more the way an editor will receive your work.	**It is harder or slower to correct misconceptions** if someone misreads your piece. There is no quick way to correct or clarify, again slowing down the process.
You can fit the critique work into your own schedule, doing it when you have time to concentrate on it. And you may get a more thorough critique because the other person is not as rushed.	**Critiques may take longer to come back**, and probably won't come in at the same time, making it harder to schedule your rewrites.
An online group might be your only option if you live in a remote area or one with few writers in your genre.	**An online group might be a cop-out for someone who is shy and doesn't want to risk relationship.** It's easy to avoid the search for an in-person group.

ADVANTAGES	DISADVANTAGES
It's easier to move on if a group doesn't meet your needs. No hard feelings. You just disappear.	**It is easier to become recluse.** It's easy to substitute your online friends for in-real-life friends.

*And let us consider
how we may spur one another on
toward love and good deeds.
Let us not give up meeting together,
as some are in the habit of doing,
but let us encourage one another —
and all the more as you see the Day approaching.*
(Hebrews 10:24–25)

How Do I Find a Group?

When you're ready to form or find a group, pray that the LORD would lead you to just the right people. Then start talking to people you know about your interest in writing. Who knows? You might already have a closet writer among your friends or acquaintances.

The best place to find a critique group is at a writers' conference. This is one of the many benefits of attending such conferences.

- ➢ Usually the conference nametags will include attendees' home city and state, so stay alert for people who live within reasonable driving distance of you.

- ➢ Ask the conference director to make an announcement to connect people looking for a critique group. Most will be happy to accommodate.

- ➢ Post your request on the conference bulletin or message board.

➤ When you find someone from your area, introduce yourself and ask if they're already part of a critique group. If so, ask if they have openings. If they're not part of a group, ask if they would be interested in starting one.

➤ Talk about what each of you writes and how serious you are.

➤ Try to spend some time together at a meal or break to get acquainted.

➤ Look for some compatibility in personality, life style, and commitment.

➤ Exchange contact information.

➤ Agree on how you will communicate when you return home.

If you can't attend a writers' conference, or just can't wait, try these methods to connect with other writers.

➤ **The Christian Writers' Market Guide is** now online (christianwritersmarketguide.com) and available for an annual subscription. In addition to all the up-to-the-moment market information, it contains an exhaustive list of writers' conferences and local writers' groups. Contact those in your area for leads.

➤ **Post a notice** in your local Christian bookstore, library, churches, coffee shops, the bulletin board outside the writing department at your local college, or even on Craigslist. You'll need a process to carefully vet potential members to determine if they are a good fit for your needs.

➤ **Your city may already have critique or writing groups**. Do a quick Internet search with your city and "writing groups" or "critique groups." Attend the group, meeting, or class to see if it might be a good fit.

➤ **Professional associations** have chapters throughout the country. Check their sites for directories to find other members in your local area. Here are some specialized associations to check:

- American Christian Fiction Writers (acfw.com),

- Mystery Writers of America (mysterywriters.org),

- Romance Writers of America (rwa.org).

➢ **You can find a more comprehensive list of writers' associations at Writer's Relief** (writersrelief.com/writers-associations-organizations). Note that this resource lists both Christian and secular groups.

➢ **Search social media and the Internet** for online groups. Either join, or ask for leads to local writers. Try these for a start:

- Facebook Groups for Writers (thewritelife.com/facebook-groups-for-writers),

- LinkedIn Groups for Writers (writerswin.com/the-real-power-of-linked-in-for-authors),

- Twitter Lists for Writers (thewritelife.com/the-15-best-twitter-lists-for-writers),

- Goodreads Writing Groups (goodreads.com/group/show_tag/writing).

- Many of these groups are also listed in *The Christian Writers' Market Guide* (christianwritersmarketguide.com/).

➢ **Pray** that God would lead you to other writers interested in becoming part of a group. The best groups are always those he puts together. You will be amazed at how quickly you come to love one another, even when you start as strangers.

---

*If you have any encouragement from
being united with Christ,
if any comfort from his love, if any
fellowship with the Spirit,
if any tenderness and compassion,
then make my joy complete by being like-minded,
having the same love, being one in spirit and purpose.*
(Philippians 2:1-2)

Who Will Lead Us?

Groups form in many ways, but ultimately someone needs to be in charge. This leadership can be formal or informal, but it needs to be there and be understood by the members. In some groups, one or two people start the group and assume leadership. In other groups, several people come together to start the group, but elect, draft, or appoint a leader.

I suggest that a group have a leader and a co-leader. This will assure that someone is in charge, as well as provide some help for that person and back up for absences. I prefer this structure to having two equal co-leaders. Ultimately, someone needs to be in charge.

Here are some of the roles of the leader and co-leader. Most of these can be distributed according to the gifts and preferences of the personalities. Basically, you want to divide responsibilities in a way that will work.

> **Call and schedule the meeting.** Although members will have the regular meeting dates on their calendars, it never hurts to

send out an email reminding them the date, time, and location of the meeting.

➢ **Request RSVPs by a specific date**. This is especially important if you are reading at the meeting so members know how many copies to bring. If your group reads and critiques in advance, let members know when manuscripts are due. A head count is also important for the host or hostess so they can plan accordingly.

➢ **Lead the meeting, including keeping track of the time schedule.** Someone needs to keep the meeting moving and transition from one activity to the next.

➢ **Work out personality differences and nurture relationships.** Hopefully this won't be a big issue, but over time, there will be hurt feelings, personality differences, and prickly people. (See "Handling Conflict," p. 69)

➢ **Identify when organizational changes need to be made.** This may include adding members, changing format, or addressing elements that aren't working. Someone must take the initiative to keep the group running smoothly.

And in the church God has appointed ...,
those with gifts of administration, ...
(1 Corinthians 12:28)

That All-Important First Meeting

Your first meeting is very important. Obviously, the person assuming leadership will have done a lot of groundwork prior to the meeting. You will have invited people, found a date that works for everyone, and begun to define the group. Now everyone is together in one location—looking at you. What do you do?

Here are the important elements in this first meeting:

> **Welcome and introduce members to one another.** If people don't know one another, consider name tags.

> **Start on time**, or close to on time. Let people know that in the future you will start on time. Latecomers should come in quietly without interrupting.

> **Take time to get acquainted.** Spend a few minutes per person learning who they are, where they live, what they write, and perhaps a bit about their families. Your goal here is to begin building trust and even affection

among members. Useful conversation starters might include:

- Who are you?

- What are you writing?

- What's your passion?

- What do you hope to gain from the group?

- What are your fears or obstacles?

- How do you want us to help you?

- What skills and gifts do you bring to the group?

➢ **Discuss the ground rules.** As the leader, you may want to decide in advance which items are pre-determined and which are open to discussion. By the end of the first meeting, you will want to have agreed upon the basic structure of the group. You may want to sign an agreement to avoid conflict later. (See "Sample Critique Group Agreement," p. 103.)

➢ **Lead the group in prayer requests and prayer.** If prayer is going to be part of your group, you may want to set the expectations for how long people share, what types of requests the group will pray for, and make sure you actually leave time to pray. This component can easily get away from you. Decide how prayer fits into your group. However, this is a place you might want to be flexible if possible. Our current group initially agreed upon one half hour for sharing and prayer. We quickly realized that in this group of praying women, we need an hour or more. Fortunately, we had the flexibility to make these changes.

➤ **Stress confidentiality.** Anything shared in the group stays in the group and is not to be discussed outside of the group. This will become important to help your group develop trust.

➤ **Make sure people know when and where the group will meet again, as well as any expectations for that meeting.** Hopefully you can schedule several months of meetings at the first meeting so people can get them on their calendars.

What then shall we say, brothers?
When you come together, everyone has a hymn,
or a word of instruction, a revelation,
a tongue or an interpretation.
All of these must be done for the
strengthening of the church.
(1 Corinthians 14:26)

Ground Rules that Make a Difference

I f you're forming a new group, you'll want to agree in advance what kind of group you'll be. While I can suggest guidelines and recommendations, the best group is one that will work for you and the other members who have decided to partner together. I suggest you use this book to establish the agenda for your first meeting and group life.

Discuss each item and come to some agreements. Note that if one person is particularly uncomfortable with guidelines that everyone else is happy with, it may be better for him or her to start or find another group rather than trying to make your group become all things to all people.

Critique groups offer more than critique. Because writing is such a personal and vulnerable exercise, members often become close. The group becomes as much a support group as a critique group. Therefore, you may prefer a group of people who are much like you—same sex, age range, marital status—so that you feel comfortable sharing deeply. Or, you may prefer a group that is very different from you so that you can gain experience with and the insights of a wider range of people. There is no right or wrong answer.

As you talk about what kind of group you'll have, it's a good idea to write down your agreements so there won't be confusion later. Of course, you can always modify the agreements as your group grows and changes. In fact, it's a good idea to revisit the agreements every year or two, just to make sure everyone is still on the same page. (A Sample Agreement is provided on page 103.)

Here are some of the decisions that you'll want to consider as you form your group. Some will be critical; others won't be important to anyone. You don't want too many rules, but a common understanding is always helpful.

Who

> **Who are we?** Perhaps the most important decision is whether you will be a Christian group or if that doesn't matter. If your members are writing for the Christian market, you will find a more empathetic and knowledgeable critique base if the group is limited to Christians. Furthermore, some groups have found that they prefer to not expose

themselves to the content written by some non-Christians.

➤ **Who's in charge?** You need to have someone in charge, but what does that mean? It may mean that this is Joe's group and he makes all the decisions. It may mean that Joe is the organizer, but everyone has a vote. At a minimum, it means that Joe sends out the reminders and serves as timekeeper. (See the chapter "Who Will Lead Us," p. 24, for more on this.)

➤ **Do we want a group with different skills levels or a group of peers?** If you are writing for publication, you will probably want a group limited to others seeking publication. Hobbyists tend to have different priorities. However, it can be good to have members with different skills and skill levels. In fact, it's exciting to mentor an inexperienced but serious writer.

➤ **How many people do we want in the group?** This will depend on how much time you want to devote to critiquing. On average, if you have a three-hour meeting and want to include prayer time and a bit of social time, and if everyone is reading almost every time, you'll want no more than six people. Assume a minimum of 20 minutes per critique if people are submitting approximately 1500 words. If you have less time available, you might need a smaller group, although critiques will suffer if you have too few. After much trial and error, we found that three hours twice per month worked well for our group of five or six.

➤ **Do we want both men and women, or only one gender?** If the group is to be a strong support and prayer group, some people feel more comfortable in a same gender group. Others don't care and adapt accordingly. This decision may also depend on the type of writing the members are doing. If the target audiences of all members are women, having men in the group won't add value. However, if members are writing for a general audience, it may be important to have both men and women in the group.

➤ **Do we have an age preference?** Some people prefer a group close in age. This is usually less important than deciding on a same-gender or mixed group. In fact, it's encouraging to have some younger people, especially if they are also new writers. However, a person of a different generation may not "get" your writing or you theirs, so you may need to recognize that in your critiques. For example, Boomers may not understand the nuances of a Gen X or Millennial writer. That doesn't make the work "wrong" or "off target." It makes it different. You'll want to be careful as you consider the writings of those in a different demographic.

➢ **Do we care about marital status?** This is usually not a concern, but be sure to ask the question.

➢ **Is this an open or closed group?** An open group means that anyone can join and usually, anyone can attend at any time. Attendance requirements are usually more flexible. With an open group, you probably won't set a size limit. You also will have less discretion about other criteria. You will also find less continuity in an open group, so if you are reading a chapter per meeting from your book, casual attenders may lack context to give you a strong critique.

A closed group is limited to those people invited or admitted based on some predetermined criteria. Closed groups develop more continuity, closeness, and confidentiality, and can more easily specify age and sex criteria.

➤ **How does one become a member, and how does one leave? (Who can invite new members—and how?)** This question applies primarily to closed groups. It stands to reason that if a group is closed, there needs to be agreement about how new members are added. Usually members discuss *if* they are open to adding a member, and if so, *who* that might be. If one member knows of someone who might be a good addition, he or she brings the name up for discussion rather than simply inviting the person to attend. In some cases, the leader makes the decisions. Just be sure you agree in advance how members are added.

➤ **What about children? (Are they allowed at the meetings?)** Unless yours is an unusual group, you won't want children in the meeting. After all, if this is a professional group, children will be a distraction. But some people won't even assume this unless it's discussed and specified. And what about emergencies? Can little Susie come and read in the corner? Depends... Discussing this in advance will avoid hurt feelings later.

> **How, if at all, do we involve spouses and families?** Some groups host one or two dinners per year where spouses were included. These are a lot of fun and give spouses a chance to meet the other writers that we spend so much time with. Other groups don't have this interest, especially if not all the members are married or if they have young children at home. This change may change over time.

WHAT

> **What is the purpose of our group?** Critique only? Study and skills development? Writing together? Support and fellowship? Prayer? Writing to heal? These are all appropriate purposes. Talk about it and make sure that you agree in advance.

> **What critique method will we adopt?** There are two popular methods of conducting critiques. One is to print out a copy of the

manuscript for each member and have the author read it aloud during the meeting. The other method is to email manuscripts out in advance. Recipients print out the manuscripts, critique at home prior to the meeting, and bring the marked-up copy to the meeting for discussion. These options are discussed in more detail in the chapter "Decide How You Will Present Material," page 49.

➢ **What does a regular meeting look like?** Again, there is no right answer here. Our original group met for three hours. Two of those hours were devoted to critiques, with about one half hour of socializing in the beginning (to allow for late-comers) and about one half hour at the end for prayer. Our current group learned at the first meeting that we need a lot more time for prayer. Other groups begin with a teaching time, then do critiques. They may or may not include time for prayer. It's truly up to you to decide as a group what you want to include or exclude.

➢ **Will we only critique at meetings or also by email between meetings?** It's important to agree on this in advance. There will be members who always have an emergency and always need a special critique. Are you willing to do this or not? Or perhaps you agree that members will try, but are under no obligation to do an extra critique.

➢ **Will there be dues or other costs associated with the group?** Most small, home-based groups don't need finances so don't charge dues. Larger groups may have administrative, location, or web expenses and therefore charge dues. Dues are also a way of assuring that only those who are serious writers join the group. But do make sure that the dues are for value-added services.

➢ **Other?** What else is important to your group?

WHEN

➢ **How often will we meet?** This may depend on how many members you have and how long you meet each time. And that, of course, depends on the time you have available. It may also depend on how far people are driving to attend. Do you want one longer meeting or several shorter meetings?

➢ **What time? What days?** This will be based on many factors. Do members work during the day? Do they have childcare responsibilities during the day? Since some in our first group had children at home, we began meeting at night. But we found that the person who got the 9:00 critique got a more yawns than help. We finally decided that since this was a professional group, it deserved our best hours. We moved to midday and had much better critiques. It's usually easiest to schedule a regular date like the first and third Monday so members can get these meetings on their calendar for the year. If you wait and schedule at each meeting, you'll never find a date everyone can make. Realize, too, that when you begin, people may have prescheduled events. That will mean that attendance in the early months could be more irregular than once the group is up and running.

➢ **How many members make a quorum?** Some groups find it isn't worth meeting if at least a minimum number of members can't attend, particularly if people are looking for a strong critique. Your leader will be the point person who receives the RSVPs and can make the call if a meeting is to be cancelled.

➤ **How do we handle absences? Occasional? Regular?** Sure, there will always be absences, and most can't be helped—sickness, travel, mother-in-law in town…. But it's important to stress your attendance expectations early on. You'll find that as you jell as a group, any absence is felt. Something (someone) is missing. However, you'll also find that once some members start skipping for non-urgent reasons, it will be easier for others to do the same. Soon you'll have a group of people who come when they don't have anything better to do. It's just human nature.

➤ If some members are consistently inconsistent, it may suggest that they aren't as committed as the other members or simply aren't in a place in their life where they can make the required commitment. You'll want a policy agreement *before* this becomes a problem. Otherwise, the offender will feel singled out.

> ➤ Another problem is the person who comes late, wants to jump to the front of the line for critique, and then needs to leave early. Yes, you will eventually have that person. You'll need to agree in advance how you want to handle such a case.

> ➤ **Other?**

WHERE

> ➤ **Where will we meet?** You can meet at a home, a restaurant, a church, or almost anyplace. In general, you want a place that offers quiet and privacy. Many restaurants will charge if you want a private room, or at a minimum, you will need to order food. You'll need to decide if you are willing to spend that money and have the added interruption of food service. Generally, a home or room at a church is your best bet. For safety reasons, consider that you might not want to meet in a home if yours is an open group. At a minimum, you'll want to take some precautions to not publicize the address on social media.

> ➤ **Will we have one location or rotate?** This is entirely a personal decision, but if you

rotate, make sure someone is responsible for reminding members where we'll be this week.

> **Are there obstacles to some locations (access, children, allergies, etc.)?** There may be reasons why some locations aren't good. Consider traffic, parking, safety, and distance. Consider which homes have children and which don't. Consider if anyone is allergic to pets.

> **Other?**

WHY

> **Critique written work.** Obviously, this is your reason for existence. If you aren't actively critiquing, you probably have a different type of group.

> **Accountability.** Perhaps one of the most important functions of a critique group is to hold members accountable to write and keep on writing. We affectionately nicknamed our first group the "butt-in-chair" group because we all needed accountability to keep writing. However, we also realized that sometimes life comes crashing in and a person simply can't

produce for every meeting or sometimes for many meetings. I had a season of over a year when I was barely writing, but I continued to attend to help my fellow writers and to remind myself that someday I would be productive again. Other groups take the position that deadlines are a critical part of the writing life. They have the policy that if you don't submit a piece to critique, you can't attend. Groups with this policy believe it motivates members to keep writing regularly. Ultimately the decision is yours, but be sure to discuss this to avoid misunderstandings later.

➢ **Helps you find your blind spots.** As writers, we all have blind spots. We think we're good at something when truth be told, we stink. We think we stink at something when in reality, we're pretty good. Or we have the potential to be pretty good once the problem is pointed out to us. After that blind spot is pointed out a few times, hopefully we become aware of it as we write.

➢ **Makes you tougher, less sensitive, and more professional.** If you want to be a professional writer, you'll need to develop a thick skin.

You won't survive if you don't. Learning how to graciously give and receive critique will help you toughen up and be a pro.

➢ **Encouragement, prayer, support, friendship, and camaraderie.** Writing is a lonely profession. Many groups consider these to be as important as critiquing. As our current group has jelled, these aspects have become as important as critiquing. Our prayer times have become rich and transformational as we listen to the LORD for one another. We are serious warriors for one another.

➢ **Education or professional development.** Some groups provide writing education, conferences, and other professional development opportunities. Will you do this during regular meetings, at other times, or not at all?

➢ **Market information.** All groups provide some market information, but some make this one of their purposes.

➢ **Other?**

HOW (SAMPLE MEETING PLAN)

> **Decide the order of readers.** It may be helpful to decide the order of readers in advance so you don't waste time figuring that out at the beginning of the meeting. Some groups require an RSVP, with reading slots determined on a first in, first out basis. Some base it on individual deadlines. Some people will be willing to go to the back of the line if they aren't on deadline. Usually the leader or co-leader will set the schedule. Do this in advance and based on agreed-upon criteria.

> **Start on time.** If you wait until everyone arrives, each subsequent meeting will start later than the previous one. This is where the leader is important. When it's time to start, start. And don't stop when latecomers arrive. Leave the door unlocked and tell members to come in quietly and settle in. Don't stop to catch them up. When they know you're serious, they'll show up on time.

> **Quick check-in.** Here is your "fudge" to the above. Consider scheduling the first 15 to 25 minutes for catch up. After all, we can't just come in and go to work, can we? This

also allows a person who is struggling with a personal issue to get it out immediately rather than being distracted through the meeting. It also allows a bit of flex for the latecomers, but don't go back and repeat for the stragglers. Some groups postpone this to the end, allowing those who need to leave to duck out.

> **Refreshments—scheduled or pot luck.** Some groups consider refreshments optional. Others consider them mandatory, and chocolate is assumed. Some groups decide no one needs one more responsibility. Members will bring refreshments when they can. No pressure. It's up to you. Just decide.

> **Read and critique manuscripts.** This is what you're here for, but it will get squeezed if someone doesn't take charge. Be sure to allow the time agreed upon for critique, divided as agreed upon. Some groups use a timer. Others just use a vigilant leader. And there is usually grace for a small fudge factor.

> **Share and prayer.** Writing is a lonely profession, and one that even our families often don't understand well. It's important to have

like-minded people with whom to share and pray. Some groups limit sharing and prayer requests to writing related needs; others are open to whatever is affecting the members. Be sure that you don't consume the time with sharing, leaving no time for prayer. Again, the leader needs to keep things moving.

➢ **End on time.** Just as it's important to start on time, so it's important to end on time. Having a firm ending time allows people to plan their day or evening. And it honors the commitment of those who attend.

Do nothing out of selfish ambition or vain conceit, but in humility consider others better than yourselves. Each of you should look not only to your own interests, but also to the interests of others. (Philippians 2:3–4)

THE CRITIQUE PROCESS

Decide How You Will Present Material

f you are meeting in person, there are two generally accepted approaches for handling critiques.

READ IN THE MEETING

One is for each writer to print out enough copies of his or her manuscript for each person expected to be in attendance. At the meeting, the writer reads the manuscript aloud. Listeners (critiquers) mark up the manuscript as they listen, and then take turns sharing their observations. Generally spelling, punctuation, and other copy edits are simply marked without discussion. There is usually a pre-determined time assigned to each critique. At the end of the critique, members put their name on their marked-up copy and return it to the reader.

Some of the advantages and disadvantages of this approach include:

TABLE 3: ADVANTAGES AND DISADVANTAGES READING IN THE MEETING

ADVANTAGES	DISADVANTAGES
The writer will experience the audience's fresh reaction. This is how the reader or editor will most likely respond to the submission.	**It may be difficult for a critiquer to catch everything in a single pass** or to render as thorough a critique as if he had more time.
The writer will catch flow and sentence structure problems that are only evident when a piece is read aloud.	**The writer may add vocal embellishments** that an editor or reader won't include.
This process will reduce the total amount of time members spend critiquing the work of others.	**The oral reading process may limit the number of manuscripts** that can be handled in a meeting.

SUBMIT MANUSCRIPTS IN ADVANCE

The other way to handle critiques is for each writer to email manuscripts out in advance. Members are expected to do their critiques before the meeting and only discuss major issues at the meeting. Again, each critiquer puts his or her name on the manuscript and returns it to the writer.

Some of the advantages and disadvantages of this approach include:

TABLE 4: ADVANTAGES AND DISADVANTAGES
OF SUBMITTING MANUSCRIPTS IN ADVANCE

ADVANTAGES	DISADVANTAGES
This approach **may allow for more members or slightly shorter meeting times.**	**It generally requires more total time from each critiquer**—first to read and critique, and then to comment in group. This can more than double the time investment of each member in the group.

ADVANTAGES	DISADVANTAGES
Members *may* be able to spend more time on a manuscript.	Members will generally need a few minutes to get back up to speed on a manuscript, especially if more than a day or two has elapsed since doing the review.
	People may not attend if they haven't done their "homework."
Critiquers make entirely independent assessments, without the influence of listening to other critiques.	The writer doesn't experience the fresh reaction of the critiquers, and the critiquers may overthink the process. An editor will seldom give you more than his or her first impression.

Ultimately, your group will decide which approach it prefers. And it may change the process from time to time as needed.

The LORD responded:
"Write down this message!
Record it legibly on tablets,
so the one who announces it may read it easily."
(Habakkuk 2:2 NET)

Do's and Don'ts for Your Meetings

Do

> ➤ **Do decide on how your group will operate and stick to those guidelines.** (See the chapter, "Ground Rules that Make a Difference," p. 31.)

> ➤ **Do get a baby sitter.** Treat your critique time as work. If you wouldn't bring your children to work, don't bring them to critique group—unless everyone has agreed to allow children at the meeting.

> ➤ **Do eliminate other distractions.** Let voice-mail answer the phone. Turn off cells phones. Put pets in another room. Turn off music. This is work time.

> ➤ **Do keep your meetings informal and relaxed,** but have a schedule and stick to it.

> ➤ **Do expect members to arrive on time and plan to stay to the end.** You want to be fair to all concerned.

➢ **Do plan reading time so that everyone has equal time or the time they need.** Cooperate with the time limits and be sensitive to others. If a person has more than one item to read, you might have them read one at the beginning and one after others have had a turn.

➢ **Do designate a timekeeper to ensure a fair division of time** if time is limited.

➢ **Do allow enough time so that each person can read an entire article or chapter.** Reading only part of a piece will generally result in a less effective critique. If you consistently run out of time, you'll need to adjust membership or meeting time. Some groups impose a word count—usually 1,500 words. This can be problematic if it's less than a full article or chapter. Discuss in advance and decide how you'll handle submission length.

➢ **Do stay alert to potential markets or resources for your fellow members.** As you read, consider if a magazine or publisher that isn't perfect for you might be for another member. Bring sample copies of magazines or similar books to share with one another. Share your CDs, books, and other writing resources.

➤ **Do celebrate your successes**—a finished book, a publication, a contract, and one another. Cooperate in launch parties and celebrate publications with lunch or chocolate.

Don't

➤ **Don't stay home because you have nothing to read.** Yes, life does come crashing in. There will be weeks or even seasons where you can't write. You can still help your fellow group members by your critiques, and attending the meeting can inspire you to go home and write. You might want to decide in advance how many meetings non-readers can attend if this is an issue for your group.

➤ **Don't let everyone talk at once**—take turns! If everyone tries to talk at the same time, it can feel like an attack on the writer. Again, the leader is critical here.

➤ **Don't let challenging people take over.** If you have challenging people or situations in your group, you may need help in dealing with them. Otherwise, it's easy for them to take over and ruin the flow of the group. A useful resource is my book, *Why Didn't You Warn Me? How to Deal with Challenging Group Members*, available at Mighty Oak Ministries (mightyoakministries.com/products/branches/smallgrouphelp.html). This book addresses eighteen common problems in small groups and provides step-by-step suggestions for handling those issues. Hopefully you'll never need it!

Iron sharpens iron,
and one person sharpens the wits of another.
(Proverbs 27:17 NRSV)

Do's and Don'ts for Readers

The guidelines below are for groups that read each manuscript aloud. You can adapt as necessary for groups that read and critique in advance. (See "Decide How You Will Present Material," p. 49.)

Do

> ➢ **Do print enough copies of your manuscript so that each member present will have one**. As a courtesy, let everyone know if you won't be there so they don't waste copies.

> ➢ **Do make sure your manuscript is double spaced and has margins wide enough for the critiquers to write notes**. Whether you use bold, italics, and other formatting functions depends on your target market. Most publishers don't want such formatting, but for critique it's less important and in fact, might be helpful. Just be sure you know the proper submission format when you get to that point.

> ➢ **Do introduce your reading with a sentence or two about the market you're targeting.**

Mention anything that will help critiquers know if you've hit the mark.

➤ **Do tell your reviewers what type of critique you want.** Beginners may want a gentler critique than experienced professionals. If you're submitting a draft, you may simply want your concept critiqued. Or perhaps you want just one element critiqued, such as character, pace, or sequencing. If you're ready for submission, you may want a strong line and copy edit. You may want the group to be tough. Just make sure you really want what you're asking for.

➤ **Do read your manuscript aloud.** Often you can catch flow, sequence, and wording problems when you hear yourself reading. If you stumble, so will your readers. Sometimes you'll read a word that isn't there or skip a word that is there. Have your listeners note when they catch such a stumble. This may suggest a better way of phrasing your sentence. You can decide later, but you'll know what your brain saw.

➤ **Do read slowly enough** that your listeners can understand, absorb, and make notes.

➤ **Do listen for vocalizations and other reactions from your listeners**. Is that gasp or groan the reaction you wanted right there? Are there furrowed brows or questioning facial expressions?

➤ **Do realize that if you must explain any part of your manuscript in your group, it may not stand a chance with an editor.** This is a good place to see if you've been perfectly clear. When it reaches the editor's desk, you won't be there to explain, defend, or interpret. Your work must stand on its own.

➤ **Do listen for positive comments and really hear them.** Sometimes it's easier to hear the criticism rather than the affirmations. Be sure you let the compliments penetrate your defenses.

➤ **Do take the stack of critiques home and pray about how you will make changes—** if at all. Chances are, you'll see the comments more objectively the next day.

DON'T

> ➤ **DON'T BECOME DEFENSIVE.** This is perhaps the most important instruction of the entire book! Do. Not. Become. Defensive! Listen with an open mind to how your work was received and interpreted by the other members. You don't need to explain or defend it. Just smile and say, "Thank you." You can decide later whether to implement each suggestion. If you become prickly at every comment, fellow members will begin to treat you with kid gloves and you won't get a critique that can help you improve.

> ➤ **Don't be surprised if different members see your work differently.** This will help you see how different types of readers will interpret your published work. A wise writer will try, to the extent possible, to eliminate any confusion or red herrings for all readers, not just for the target audience.

> ➤ **Don't assume that your work is inspired or dictated by God.** Don't blame God for your errors or weaknesses. As a writer, *you* are responsible for what you write and how you write it. Almost every piece will benefit

from editing by another person. Or from several other people.

➤ **Consider the rule of three:** Assume that if three people make the same comment, or type of comment, there is probably some validity to it.

➤ **Don't get discouraged.** Not everything you bring will be a winner, but over time, solid critiques can help make you a better writer. One group literally rewrote books or major sections of books. But in the process, the writer learned and became a better writer.

➤ **Don't feel you must accept every comment.** It's your work and ultimately your responsibility.

Wounds from a friend can be trusted,
but an enemy multiplies kisses.
(Proverbs 27:6)

Do's and Don'ts for Critiquers

Do

➤ **Do mark up each manuscript as you read it or as the reader reads it.** Use ink or a pencil that is dark enough to be easily seen. You might consider not using a red pen unless everyone agrees it's OK. Sometimes a red pen mark-up can remind the reader of that sixth-grade teacher who never liked their work. On the other hand, our group likes red pens. Just ask.

➤ **Do vocalize your emotional reactions** while the writer is reading. A spontaneous gasp, groan, or laugh will tell the writer if she has hit the mark. In fact, you might want to exaggerate this just a bit, especially if you are normally a silent listener. (But don't comment—see next tip.) Mark your reaction in the margins—"Yes!" "Good!" "Wow!" "Love this!"

➤ **Do hold comments to the end.** Don't interrupt the flow of the reading. Mark up your copy of the manuscript as you listen, and then use those notes to give your verbal critique. Often a question you have will be answered during the remainder of the reading.

➢ **Do give positive comments first.** Start by finding something that you like about the piece. If possible, give several positives before starting with the suggestions. Give your suggestions and then finish with another positive. We all need affirmation. And be sure that you write the positive comments on the manuscript so they don't get lost in in the discussion.

➢ **Do keep comments constructive, kind, and loving.** Remember that this is someone's "baby" you're talking about. Don't call it ugly! Let your aim be to help, not to be critical.

➢ **Do remain sensitive to body language and receptivity.** You may be right, but you may need to back off. It isn't your responsibility to force your ideas on the writer. Stay alert for hurt feelings, envy, and comparisons. Back off if necessary. Realize that, "I want a tough critique," may not mean what you think it means.

➢ **Do try to offer alternatives rather than just saying something doesn't work.** This isn't always possible, but chances are, the writer will appreciate your efforts to suggest a fix. However, don't think that you need to rewrite the piece for the writer. Ultimately, the writer has that responsibility. Use good judgment as you work with both beginners, who might need a bit of hand-holding, and more experienced writers, who can take your comments and run with them.

➢ **Do use tentative language as you offer your critique.** For example, instead of saying, "You need to change the second sentence...," say something like, "*I wonder if* that second sentence *could be* improved by saying *something like...*" or "*It seems to me* you have two conflicting thoughts in that second sentence..." That allows the reader to consider your remarks as a suggestion rather than a mandate, a critique rather than a criticism.

➢ **Do give a more exacting critique to a professional than to a beginner.** Try to tailor your critique to the level of the writer, understanding that a beginner will not reach the same level as the published professional. But at the same time, strive to bring each writer to their highest level possible.

➢ **Do return your marked-up manuscript to the reader.** You may want to make spelling, punctuation, and grammar suggestions on the manuscript without taking group time to discuss them. Put your name or initials on the manuscript so the writer knows who made the comments.

➢ **Do make suggestions for potential markets or different slants.** You may have ideas for refocusing or repurposing the work that the author didn't think about.

DON'T

➢ **Don't overwhelm.** Gauge how much needs to be said and how much the writer is willing to hear. Consider making some comments or suggestions in writing without verbal comment if you sense the reader is becoming overwhelmed.

➤ **Don't assume that your comments must be implemented.** Present them as suggestions. A wise writer will consider constructive comments, but is under no obligation to follow them.

➤ **Don't engage in a debate or argue the author's thesis or minor doctrinal differences.** This can be touchy if you don't agree with the approach or the theology, but if the piece is appropriate for the anticipated market, critique it accordingly.

➤ **Don't avoid making constructive criticism, even if it means saying that something is not ready to publish.** Your group is not a mutual admiration society, but rather a group of professional Christian artists seeking to improve their craft. If your goal is to help everyone improve his or her writing, your criticism must be honest. Sensitive, but honest.

➤ **Don't change the voice of the writer.** While he may not say it like you would, does it make sense? Does it work? Does it sound authentic to the writer? Work with the writer's voice.

➤ **Don't make snide or "dissing" remarks, even in jest.** Honor one another as fellow co-laborers in a difficult field.

➤ **Don't attack the writer's abilities or person.** Rather, be as objective and kind as possible in critiquing the work as presented.

➤ **Don't monopolize.** If you have more to critique than time allows, make notes on your manuscript and offer to talk to the writer privately if they wish.

Let your conversation be always full of grace, seasoned with salt, so that you may know how to answer everyone. (Colossians 4:6)

Handling Conflict

I hate to be the one to break this to you, but if your group is composed of human beings, you will have conflict. Sooner or later, someone will offend or be offended. Sooner or later, someone will consistently violate the agreements you've agreed to. Sooner or later, someone's personal issues or foibles will drive someone else crazy.[2]

WHAT DO YOU DO?

First, whether you are the offended or the offender, take a deep breath. This does not have to be the end of the group as you know it. In fact, conflict, when handled well, can deepen the trust and relationships in your group. Of course, the converse is also true. Conflict, handled poorly, can blow up and hurt a lot of people in the process.

---

[2] As one member said, "you never appreciate an agreement until you need it." In addition to the suggestions in this chapter, you'll find many more tips and strategies in Pat J. Sikora, *Why Didn't You Warn Me? How to Deal with Challenging Group Members*, Small Group Help Guides (Cincinnati, Ohio: Standard Publishing, 2007). (mightyoakministries. com/products/branches/smallgrouphelp.html).

Remember that as a writer who is a Christian, your work is an offering to God. Your conduct in the group should reflect your faith. While members of a secular group might just go away mad, as Christians, we are called to a higher standard. What might that look like in your group?

In all aspects of conflict resolution, be sure to fight fair. Let's look at some generalizations for fighting fair and then we'll look at some specifics for your group. These guidelines assume a personal discussion by the group or by two or more individuals in the group. While much of this will be orchestrated and moderated by the leader, everyone has a responsibility for the group and for making sure that everyone feels heard and validated.

FIGHT FAIR

> **Pray together.** Before discussing an issue of conflict, it's a good idea to pray, both individually and as a group. Ask God how he sees this conflict. How does he want you to grow through this? What are the bigger or unspoken issues? Be sure to not lean only on your own understanding, but rather, pray for the LORD's wisdom, grace, and direction. Feel free to stop and pray

during any discussion if you feel emotions are becoming overwhelming or if you've hit an impasse. And of course, pray at the end of the discussion, whether the issue is completely resolved or not.

➤ **Know your own feelings.** It's important that before you dive into conflict, you seek to grow in your own self-awareness. Prayerfully get in touch with your own feelings so that you can constructively handle conflict. Is your frustration with the group or a specific person? Is it perhaps displaced anger or frustration with a family member, your health, financial issues, or other problems? Does the issue or person you are feeling irritated by remind you of Mom? Knowing this will help you be more objective.

➤ **Recognize that anger is an emotion— in itself, it's neither right nor wrong.** What makes it wrong is when you take a destructive or thoughtless action because of a feeling. More important is understanding that feelings are a result of thoughts or beliefs. When you take time to understand the thoughts driving the feelings you will be better able to find creative ways to solve the problem.

➤ **Check yourself and your motives.** Is there something else going on in your life that is being deflected to the group—perhaps because it feels safer than dealing with the real issue? Don't take out your personal, relational, financial, or health issues on your group.

➤ **Recognize that negotiation and compromise are essential in any relationship—and your group is a complex relationship.** Remember that the issue is *not* one of winning or losing. If one person or side wins, the other loses and that builds resentment. In effect, both have then lost because the relationship is damaged. Even when one person is wrong, permit him or her to salvage self-respect by offering grace. Consider sandwiching a criticism between two compliments or positive statements.

➤ **Consider a cooling-off period if necessary.** Establish ground rules that permit any person in the group to "cool off" before trying to resolve an issue. It may be necessary to take a break or even schedule another meeting to allow overwhelming feelings to dissipate. This can allow members to identify the issue more clearly and organize their thoughts, thus keeping the discussion more on focus. Realize that most issues don't need to be resolved right now.

➤ **Agree to a time and place.** To assure that resolving an issue is not postponed indefinitely, agree to a time and place to continue. However, don't wait too long or you risk losing people. Whatever you do, don't "not engage."

➤ **Fight by mutual consent.** Don't insist that a problem be addressed when others are unprepared or for some reason are unable to handle the strain. A fair fight requires ready participants.

➤ **Stick to the subject.** If several issues seem to be accumulating, present them one at a time. If past issues crop up as also unresolved, put them on a current or future agenda, but don't try to solve every problem all at once.

➤ **State the issue honestly and clearly.** Express your concerns in tentative language rather than as an accusation. Tentative language is "I wonder if…" or "It seems to me…" Avoid the use of "always" and "never." Always is seldom always and never is seldom never.

➤ **Own your feelings:** Use "I" statements rather than "you" statements. "I" statements take ownership of the problem. "You" statements accuse and close the door to reconciliation. Begin with something like, "I have a concern I need to talk to you about. Is now a good time?" In the discussion, say something like, "I'm feeling…" or "I'm having a problem with…" or even "When you… I feel…." Just be careful that the "you" part doesn't sound accusatory.

➤ **Don't camouflage.** Don't evade a deeper grievance by allowing your feelings to center only on less important or extraneous issues. For example, don't complain about the refreshments if the issue is that Susan always comes late and disrupts the meeting, or that Rick always sounds harsh when he's critiquing your work.

➤ **Be Brave.** Are you afraid to fight? Almost everyone is. Own that feeling. Express your discomfort. But don't let your fear stand in the way of resolving something important to you or another group member.

> **Don't hit below the belt.** Everyone has vulnerable areas. Don't use your confidential knowledge of another person's weaknesses or sensitivities to hurt them.

> **Grant equal time.** Agree that no issue can be presumed resolved until each member has had the chance to express his or her feelings, ideas, information, observations, or solutions.

> **Clarify by using active listening.** If the dispute is getting emotional and heated, slow it down by starting a "feedback loop." Paraphrase back to the speaker what you heard. For example, "Susan, what I hear you saying is that you feel group members don't take your writing as seriously as we take that of others. Am I understanding you correctly?" Susan then responds by either confirming the accuracy of your statement or by clarifying it. Continue until you are certain that everyone is being heard accurately.

> **Implement changes.** Follow a discussion with a fair, firm, clear request for change or improvement in whatever brought on the dispute. Each person must be clear as to what he or she will agree to change or improve. Be specific and realistic.

> **Use humor.** Humor can go a long way towards promoting healing, but only if used with sensitivity. Be sure to avoid sarcasm and caustic humor.

> **Respect crying.** Crying is often a valid expression of how we feel. However, don't let crying sidetrack you from getting to the real issue causing the conflict.

Now let's look at some specifics on how to handle conflict within your group from both sides.

IF YOU ARE FEELING OFFENDED

> **Pray!** Before you say or do anything, take your concerns to the LORD. Are your frustrations reasonable? How would someone else interpret them? Ask the LORD and listen for his still small voice. Look for an indication of how God sees this issue.

➤ **Check yourself and your motives.** See the above discussion on fair fighting. Also ask yourself, "Is it worth it?" Not everything is equally important. Choose your battles wisely.

➤ **Get a second opinion.** Sometimes our perceptions can be skewed by any number of factors. Share your concern with your leader, or if the leader is the problem, with another group member. Make sure that your attitude is one of reconciliation, not gossip. The purpose of this discussion is not to build an alliance or "gang up" on another member. It's simply to see if there might be another way of looking at your concern.

➤ **Communicate in person if possible,** by phone if an in-person meeting isn't going to work. Avoid email or text if possible. We all read body language and tone of voice as part of effective communication and you can't gain the benefit of these indicators in electronic communication. The more aspects of these clues you remove from your communication, the more likely you will be misunderstood and even risk offending others. We think that a quick email or text is a good way to avoid conflict, but it usually increases the misunderstanding. While written words of affirmation or encouragement can be reread and cherished, written words of criticism or anger will also be reread, but will have a negative effect and increase the problem rather than solve it.

> **Go to the offender quickly (Matthew 18:15-17).** Express your concerns in tentative language rather than as accusation and using "I" statements rather than "you" statements (see "Own Your Feelings" above). Begin with something like, "I have a concern I need to talk to you about. Is now a good time?" If it isn't, schedule a time that works for both of you.

> **If the offense is with the whole group,** ask the leader to set aside time in the schedule at the next meeting to discuss the issue. At the meeting, express your concerns using "I" statements and tentative language. Remain open to the possibility that your perception is skewed. Be willing to hear and consider other input.

IF YOU ARE THE PERCEIVED OFFENDER (OR ONE OF THEM)

> ➤ **Pray!** When you become aware of a problem and before you say or do anything, take your concerns to the LORD. Are the complaints or frustrations reasonable? How would someone else interpret them? Ask the LORD and listen for his still small voice. Look for an indication of how God sees this issue.

> ➤ **Check yourself and your motives.** See the above discussion on fair fighting.

> ➤ **Go quickly when you become aware someone is offended by or upset by you.** Matthew 5:23-24 puts the responsibility on both parties to move toward reconciliation. Go in person if possible. By phone if an in-person meeting would delay resolution. Avoid email and text whenever possible. Encourage both parties to use fair fighting techniques (above). Seek an objective third party if appropriate. Of course this is uncomfortable, but it's oh so worth it!

REGARDLESS OF YOUR POSITION

> ➤ **Recognize that everyone is under pressure.**
> Almost everyone these days is staggering under the stress of a deadline or life situations that impact their writing. That may lead one or more people to feel frustrated or unsupported by another person or the whole group in one way or another. Make sure that everyone understands what you have agreed to and that, as much as possible, people are living up to those agreements.

> ➤ **Remember that people are different.**
> Recognize the personality differences in the group, and to the extent possible, celebrate them. Others in your group will not see things as you do or handle pressures as you do. Some are quiet, never expressing a concern. Others are more vocal, even high drama at times. Some are direct; others are more reserved. Just because a person doesn't react as you would like or expect, don't discount their feelings. And make sure that the frustration of the offended person is not just a difference of personalities.

➢ **Celebrate each person's uniqueness.** Yes, it's possible that you are a better writer or editor than someone else in the group. Or they are better than you. Maybe you're the technology guru. Maybe you're a walking encyclopedia of theology. Maybe you're the ray of sunshine when others are feeling discouraged. Bottom line is that everyone is strong in some areas and weak in others. You can form resentments, or you can celebrate the uniqueness of each person and value what they bring to the group. I hope you'll choose the latter.

➢ **Seek reconciliation, not victory.** As mentioned above, your goal must be restoration of the relationship, not a win. If others have offended you, seek reconciliation and restoration.

➢ **Reiterate applicable portions of your group agreement.** Be open to modification if that will work for everyone, but hopefully you considered most options when you signed the agreement. Be careful about amending it every time someone is unhappy. At the same time, see if there are any reasonable accommodations that can be made to make the group work better if necessary.

> **Apologize quickly when you are wrong.** If others apologize, accept it quickly and graciously.

If you need more support, there are many resources on the Internet for conflict resolution. Remember that you are not just a professional organization. You are the Body of Christ and are becoming a group of close friends who care for one another as you care for yourself. Strive to become an Acts 2 community where your skills, time, and resources are available to one another as needed and where mutual respect and admiration become the norm.

"So if you are presenting a sacrifice
at the altar in the Temple
and you suddenly remember that
someone has something against you,
leave your sacrifice there at the altar.
Go and be reconciled to that person.
Then come and offer your sacrifice to God.
(Matthew 5:23-24 NLT)

Elements to Consider In a Critique

Depending on how much time you have and what the writer wants, you can use this checklist to structure your critique. Better yet, use it to edit your own work *before* taking it to your critique group. While not every item on the checklist will apply to every piece, be sure to at least consider the major categories.[3] And of course, as a writer, you are free to break any rule. Just know *why* you are breaking it. Let the variation be stylistic, not ignorance.

> ➤ **Check for Flow and Word Count**

>> • Does the chapter, story, or article flow well?

---

[3]   These tips are explained in more detail in the book *Building Blocks of Editing* by Pat J. Sikora, available from Mighty Oak Ministries (mightyoakministries.com/products/ acorns/books/buildingblocksofediting.html). This book uses the parts of speech and basic grammatical principles as organizing tools for writing and suggests a step by step (building block by building block) approach for editing your own work or that of another. Some of these are very basic, almost elementary. But you'll be amazed at how many writers don't know or follow these rules.

- Does it seem to be in the right order?

- Is it well organized? Unified?

- Does it make sense in the order it's in? Is it believable?

- How close is it to the required or suggested word count? Can it be tightened? In a book, are the chapters about the same length unless there is good reason for variation?

➢ **Sentences**

- Does each sentence contain at least one noun or pronoun (which may be understood) and one verb?

- Does each sentence communicate a complete thought?

- Does each sentence begin with a capital letter and end with an appropriate punctuation mark?

➢ **Paragraphs**

- Does each paragraph contain only one main idea?

- Does that main idea have a sense of beginning and ending?

- Does the paragraph have a topic sentence that announces what it is about?

- Does the paragraph have one or more middle sentences that carry the action or information forward?

- Does the paragraph have an ending sentence that sums up the information?

- Is a new paragraph indicated by indenting the first line about five spaces or by skipping two spaces between paragraphs?

➤ Nouns

- Does each sentence use the strongest, most specific nouns possible?

- Is each noun as colorful and descriptive as possible?

- When appropriate, has the writer used strong nouns rather than pronouns or adjectives?

➢ **Verbs**

- Has the writer used active rather than passive verbs wherever possible?

- Has the writer used vivid action verbs to describe and advance the piece?

- Has the writer used strong verbs rather than adverbs wherever possible?

- Has the writer used creative alternatives to "said," without going overboard?

- Has the writer kept the manuscript in the same tense unless there is a good reason for a change?

- If the writer changed tense, are the transitions clear and understandable?

- Has the writer used the proper form of verb, especially irregular verbs?

➢ **Adjectives and Adverbs**

- Has the writer used the strongest nouns and verbs before resorting to adjectives and adverbs?

- Has the writer used the most vivid, most specific adjective or adverb possible?

- Has the writer used only one adjective per noun or one adverb per verb wherever possible?

- Does each adjective or adverb give new or essential information?

- Does each adjective or adverb serve a necessary purpose?

- Does the sentence flow easily when read aloud?

➤ Leads and Hooks

- Has the writer used the best lead possible?

- Is the lead compelling? Does it hook you or draw you in? Is it appropriate to the type of piece and the market?

- Does the lead make you want to continue reading?

- Is the style of the lead consistent with the purpose in writing this piece?

- Does the piece deliver what the lead promises?

➤ **Characterization**

- Are the characters realistic? You may have characters in both fiction and non-fiction.

- Are the characters or subjects described in vivid terms that will help the reader get to know them?

- Has the writer used sensory words to describe the subject?

- Has the writer used action words in combination with descriptive terms to make the subject come alive?

- Do the characters or subjects seem human?

- Has the writer been kind? Fair?

➤ **Dialogue**

- Is the dialogue realistic? Does it sound like real people talk, without being stilted or unkind?

- Did the writer remain true to any accent or dialect throughout the piece?

- When quoting people, has the writer shown them in their best light, regardless of which side of the issue they are on?

- Has the writer used creative alternatives for "said," without sounding trite or overly dramatic?

➢ **Transitions**

- Are transitions clear? Can you follow the sequence? Are time changes clear?

- Do the thoughts flow in a logical order?

- Has the writer used transition words and phrases effectively to keep the reader on track?

- Do flashbacks, dreams, and other non-sequiturs flow smoothly?

➢ **Ending Well**

- Has the writer selected the most effective style of ending for the article, chapter, or book?

- Does the ending deliver what the lead promised?

- Has the writer tied up all the loose ends?

➢ **The Title**

- Is the title interesting? Is it appropriate for the piece and the market?

- Does the title accurately reflect what follows without giving away the plot or main point of the article, chapter, or book?

- Does the title hook the reader to read the piece?

- Does the title keep the audience in mind?

➢ **The Mechanics**

- Are the vocabulary and style appropriate to the target audience?

- Has the writer double-checked every quotation, including Scripture, for accuracy?

- Has the writer used the Bible translation preferred by the publisher?

- Has the writer properly cited any work quoted or relied upon heavily?

- Are there spelling, punctuation, or capitalization errors? Be sure to look for those the spellchecker and grammar checker typically miss.

- Does the piece flow well when read aloud?

- Are there bloopers like misplaced modifiers and dangling participles?

- Are there clichés?

- Is there repetition of words or phrases within close proximity?

- Are there sentences that are too long or too short without good reason?

- Are there run on sentences or sentence fragments?

- Are there awkward sentence structures?

- Has the word count been verified and included it at the top of the manuscript if needed?

- Has the writer followed standard manuscript format and the publisher's specific guidelines for submission if needed?

➤ **The Final Check**

- Is it interesting? Do you want to keep reading to the end?

- Has the writer answered all the questions raised?

- Does it "show, not tell?" Can you see, hear, feel, taste, and smell the descriptions? The action?

- Does it matter? Would anyone care to read this? Are the ideas fresh, true, noteworthy?

- Is it preachy or condescending? Does the author have an "attitude" that comes through?

- Is the author qualified to write this? Does she have the experience, knowledge, and/ or credentials to write with credibility?

- Does the article, chapter, or story make one good point? Or does it wander off in too many directions? Is there too much or too little material for the length? Does it tie up loose ends?

- Does it reach a logical conclusion? Is the ending satisfying or are you disappointed, left wondering?

- Is it clear enough to stand on its own, without needing the author to explain anything?

- Could the writer proudly hand this to Jesus, saying, "This is what I did with the talent you gave me."

- Would He smile and reply,

...Well done, good and faithful servant!
You have been faithful with a few things;
I will put you in charge of many things.
Come and share your master's happiness!
(Matthew 25:23)

BECOMING A FULL-SERVICE GROUP

Other Activities Your Group Can Do

A s you become colleagues, you may find that other activities and functions become natural add-ons to the critique and support functions of your group. Here are some other activities that groups have added to their mix.

> ➢ **Create a closed Facebook page for your group.** This is a wonderful place to consolidate communication, upload resources, and share prayer requests. Some groups may prefer email, but a Facebook group is an option.

> ➢ **Assign members to monitor the changes in different markets.** Keep track of guidelines and staff changes using Christian Writers' Market Guide (christianwritersmarketguide.

com). Report changes at meetings, by email, or on your Facebook page.

➢ **Assign members to analyze markets of interest to the group.** Spend a few minutes at each meeting introducing markets by type or denomination. For example, if you are writing for periodicals or the Internet, compare several Sunday School take-homes or several parenting magazines. Or if you are writing historical fiction, compare the catalogs of several publishers.

➢ **Study and help one another with self-publishing.** Assign members to monitor changes in various self-publishing companies and provide support or resources to one another.

➢ **Study and help one another with marketing strategies.** Share information members have learned about resources for launching and marketing their writing. Develop a marketing support team to help with book launches. Use your networks and skills to help anyone launching a book or major project. Some groups start a separate Master Mind Group to coach one another on business and marketing strategies.

➢ **Make and maintain a list of magazines members subscribe to** or have access to through friends, relatives, or church, especially if any members are interested in writing articles.

➢ **Make and maintain a list of writing reference books, CDs, or MP3s** that members have and are willing to loan to one another.

➢ **Study a book on the writing craft together.** This is especially useful if you have several new writers or see the same types of problems repeatedly.

➢ **Invite local published writers to speak at your group,** especially those successful in the genres of your group members. Check with your local community college, university, or adult education. This might even include one of your own members.

➢ **Invite members to report on writers' conferences, book signings, local lectures or other events** they have attended.

➤ **Attend these events together.** Meet for coffee afterward to discuss what you learned.

➤ **Share writing tips, workflow, resources, and methods with one another.** Talk about overcoming writers block, writing habits, and strategies to handle problems. Learn from the strengths of your fellow members.

➤ **Conduct a group retreat.** Spend time writing together. Develop your personal mission statements and career plans. Do creative writing and art exercises. Pray. Play.

➤ **Plan and host a writers' conference or seminar.** Invite other writers you know. Advertise in churches, bookstores, and libraries.

➤ **Publish a newsletter, blog, web page, or anthology** to promote your work and share your knowledge. Offer gifts and prizes to keep your audience coming back for more.

Where there is no guidance, a people falls,
but in an abundance of counselors there is safety.
(Proverbs 11:14 ESV)

CONCLUSION

So there you have it! You now have just about everything you need to start and lead a successful critique group. All that's missing is you—and a few other members. And we even told you where to find them.

I hope you'll use this handbook to evaluate your options, to take the first step, to decide what kind of group will work for you and your members, and then to take the next steps. Come back to it when things get frustrating or confusing. They will. But the answers are here for you. In this book, you have everything you need to establish a critique group that will actually work.

And when you do that, you'll see the collective skills of your group members increase meeting by meeting, month by month, year by year. It won't happen all at once. It won't happen uniformly. Some members will take off and finish a book (or two or three) and get published quickly. Others will be slower. But the joy of an effective group is that the speedy ones, the experienced ones, the more skilled ones, gain joy from mentoring the others. And the newer writers benefit tremendously from being in relationship with the more experienced writers.

I'd love to hear from you. What's working? What isn't? Feel free to share your critique group joys and frustrations with me. Email me at pats@ mightyoakministries.com or connect with me on Facebook (facebook.com/mightyoakministries).

SAMPLE CRITIQUE GROUP AGREEMENT

As you are organizing your group and then periodically as it goes on, you may want to create and sign a group agreement. It's better to do this before there are problems than to try to implement it later. Talk about the things that are most important to your group and draft the agreement based on those. Don't try to be all-inclusive. Just cover those items that will keep problems to a minimum.

Below is a sample of one such agreement. Use it as a model or as a jumping off point for your own agreement.

Our Critique Group's Agreement
(date)

In our critique group, we focus on the whole relationship. We are more than professional colleagues; we are friends and prayer partners. We desire to grow deeper in the LORD and with one another.

In the interest of maintaining the cooperative spirit of our critique group, we the undersigned reaffirm our agreements:

> **Membership:** We are a closed (open) group of (number) of Christian women (men, members). We will only add members based on unanimous agreement or to replace a member who is leaving. We will not invite guests to attend a meeting without prior approval of all members.

> **Leadership:** The group will be led by (name), with assistance from (name). Other members will assist as needed and as they are able.

> **Meeting Time, Place, & Agenda:** We will generally meet (days) of every month from (time) to (time). We will generally meet at the home of (name), or other locations to be agreed upon from time to time. Time in the meeting will be divided into a very brief check-in, approximately (number) hours of critiques, and approximately (number) minutes of sharing and prayer. We will make every effort to begin and end on time.

➢ **Attendance:** Recognizing that each person makes a vital contribution to the group as a whole, we will make every effort to keep the meeting time free and to attend every meeting. We will make every effort to arrive on time and stay for the whole meeting. If members are traveling, they may choose to Skype into the meeting.

➢ **Notifications**: We will email our intention to attend or not, and if we are reading, approximately how many pages (words) to (leader's name and email address) no later than (when) before each meeting.

➢ **Purpose:** The primary purpose of our group will be to critique our work for publication and to hold one another accountable to continue writing. We may, from time to time, agree to other functions.

➢ **Amount to be Critiqued:** In general, we will allow approximately (number of minutes) to each person to read and receive critiques or to use for whatever other purpose he or she needs, i.e. market analysis, concept analysis, etc. The amount to be read will generally be approximately (number of words). If one or more members are not reading, these limits can be adjusted accordingly.

➤ **Approach to Critiques**: We will critique by reading our work aloud in the meeting rather than emailing it in advance. The leader will notify members how many will attend each meeting. Each person reading will print enough copies to provide one for each person attending. Manuscripts should be at least double-spaced. We will conduct our critiques with grace and sensitivity. We will mention the positive first, and seek to individually and collectively give our best to each work.

➤ **Extraordinary Critiques:** Regarding email critiques between meetings, we agree that we will do our best, but are not obligated. Those requesting the between-meeting reviews need to give as much time as possible, to indicate when the review is needed, and to do their best to not abuse the privilege. Email reviews are the exception, not the rule. There may also be occasional times when a member needs to have a complete book or document reviewed outside of meetings. We agree to make the extra effort and do this as quickly as possible, within the limits of our individual time responsibilities. These reviews will require as long a lead-time as possible.

➢ **Refreshments** will be provided on a voluntary basis. No assignments. (Or assigned and rotated among members).

➢ **Confidentiality**: We will maintain strict confidentiality in all we hear in meetings and from members.

➢ **Communication:** We will communicate primarily by email and our Facebook group at (Facebook url).

Signed _____   Date _____

Signed _____   Date _____

Signed _____   Date _____

Signed _____   Date _____

Signed _____   Date _____

Signed _____   Date _____

Signed _____   Date _____

BIBLIOGRAPHY

McPhee, John. *Draft No. 4 : On the Writing Process.* First edition. ed. New York: Farrar, Straus and Giroux, 2017.

Sikora, Pat J. *Why Didn't You Warn Me? How to Deal with Challenging Group Members* Small Group Help Guides. Cincinnati, Ohio: Standard Publishing, 2007.

www.ingramcontent.com/pod-product-compliance
Lightning Source LLC
Chambersburg PA
CBHW071236020426
42333CB00015B/1498

* 9 7 8 1 9 4 7 8 7 7 0 0 9 *